UNIT 1

A Northern Ireland

1 Jean Brady and Silke Wendt

a) Meet Jean Brady:

Age:	15
Place of birth:	Belfast
Address:	193 New Street, Belfast, Northern Ireland
School:	Lagan College, Belfast
Foreign languages:	French (four years), German (one and a half years)
Hobbies:	sports, saxophone
Best thing for her last year:	first prize in saxophone competition
Worst thing for her so far:	car accident last month; on the the way to school on her bike – dark morning – stop and wait to turn right – no lights on her bike – hit from behind by car
Plans for the next summer holidays:	shop assistant in local supermarket (three weeks), adventure holidays in the South of France (two weeks)

b) Meet Silke Wendt:

Age:	16
Place of birth:	Bautzen
Address:	66 Grossenhainer Straße, Bautzen, Germany
School:	Robert Scholtz Gymnasium, Bautzen
Foreign languages:	English (three years)
Hobbies:	pop music, computer games
Best thing for her last year:	trip to Open Air Concert in Berlin with her friend Gaby
Worst thing for her last year:	mountain bike stolen – go to music shop – leave bike in front of shop – not lock it – want to buy CD – talk to shop assistant – young man
Plans for the next summer:	on a farm (two weeks), trip through Black Forest (two weeks), computer fair in Stuttgart (one weekend)

Introduce both girls. Use full sentences with verbs and be careful with the te
Use your exercise book.

2 Beryl the Peril*

In Mr Brady's letter to Silke there was also a little note from Jean. It said:

> Dear Silke,
> In our English class last week we had to fill in a comic strip. Below you can find my solution if you can match the letters and the numbers. Don't worry: I'll let you have the solution in my next letter.
> Love, Jean

My solution:
a) Beryl has probably played a trick** on me again.
b) I'm sorry Beryl, but it seems there are only jobs for dad today.
c) I'm very tired today. Could you two do the housework for me?
d) Oh! It was lucky you were there, Dad.
e) That doesn't sound like you, Beryl.
f) Then I'll wash them and … Oops!
g) Don't worry, Mum! I'll help you!
h) First, I'll take the dishes into the kitchen…
i) Football's on now, Beryl!
j) Be careful, Beryl, you're going to fall.
k) Oh! And I wanted to help!
l) Leave the dishes, Beryl.
m) Isn't that great? I don't have anything to do. We can watch sports.
n) Will you do them for us, Dad?

1. *Do Silke's job.*

   1. ___ 2. ___ 3. ___ 4. ___ 5. ___ 6. ___   7. ___ 8. ___ 9. ___ 10. ___ 11. ___ 12. ___ 13. ___ 14. ___

2. *Report the statements, questions and orders.*
   Example: In the first picture Beryl's mother says that she…
   Go on. Do this exercise in your exercise book.

   peril ['perəl] – Gefahr
   **trick* [trɪk] – Streich

3 The invitation to Belfast

Past perfect, past perfect continuous or past tense? Write the sentences in your exercise book.

1. After / Silke / receive / the letter, / she / open / it.
2. As / she / never / have / a letter in English / before, / she / fetch / her dictionary.
3. But / she / really / not need / it / for the letter / because / Mr Brady / write / it / so that / she / be able to / read / it / easily.
4. As soon as / she / understand / that / the Bradys / invite / her to Belfast, / her heart / start / to beat faster.
5. She / secretly / always hope / for an invitation. / And now / it / be / there!
6. And / she / dream of / a trip to the British Isles / for so long!
7. It / be / as if / she / win a prize / because / she / do a lot of work / in English / since / her last school report. / It / be / very good, / too.
8. As soon as / her parents / decide / that / Silke / could / go to Belfast, / Silke / phone / her friend Gaby / and / tell her the good news.

B The peoples of the British Isles

1 Can you remember? *Read through the information on page 11 of your English book again.*

The British Isles =   England + Wales + _____

(Great) Britain = _____

Ireland = _____

The United Kingdom = _____

Wales

Part of: _____

Population: _____

Area: _____

Capital: _____

Official languages: _____

Protestants: _____

Catholics: _____

Part of: _____

Population: _____

Area: _____

Capital: _____

Official languages: _____

Protestants: _____

Catholics: _____

Northern Ireland (Ulster)

Scotland

Part of: _____

Population: _____

Area: _____

Capital: _____

Official languages: _____

Protestants: _____

Catholics: _____

Part of: _____

Population: _____

Area: _____

Capital: _____

Official languages: _____

Protestants: _____

Catholics: _____

Republic of Ireland

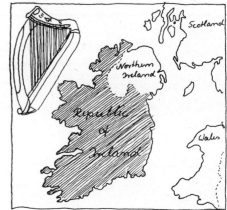

England

Part of: _____

Population: _____

Area: _____

Capital: _____

Official languages: _____

Protestants: _____

Catholics: _____

2 Why?

1. Why are the people in the British Isles mainly Christian?

   Because _____

   _____

2. Why aren't Welsh and Gaelic spoken in England?

   Because _____

   _____

3. Why did the Protestant North become richer than the Catholic South in the nineteenth century?

Because _____

4. Why did so many Irish people leave their country for the USA in the nineteenth century?

Because _____

_____

5. Why did the Irish in southern Ireland start an uprising at the beginning of the 20th century?

Because _____

_____

6. Why didn't Ulster become independent in 1921?

Because _____

7. Why did the Catholics in Northern Ireland begin to fight in the sixties?

Because _____

_____

8. Why were British soldiers brought into Northern Ireland in 1968?

Because _____

_____

3 Hidden words

Find the twelve hidden words. They have something to do with the countries of the British Isles.
You may read →, ↓ or ↑.
Then match them with the words on the right.

HOUSE OF GROUPS IRELAND
POTATO BECOME KINGDOM
CIVIL RIGHTS MINORITY
IRISH MONDAY CULTURE WAR

	a	b	c	d	e	f	g	h	i	j	k	l	m	n
1	L	T	U	M	N	Q	V	Z	V	I	J	O	R	L
2	L	N	O	R	T	H	E	R	N	T	P	S	V	M
3	N	Z	R	O	I	I	T	E	A	S	T	E	R	S
4	S	C	E	M	M	E	O	P	L	F	K	I	P	U
5	Z	A	S	A	Q	N	I	U	N	I	T	E	D	O
6	R	T	T	N	E	I	S	B	O	M	Z	V	S	I
7	Q	H	R	E	E	M	J	L	V	Y	Q	R	N	G
8	B	O	I	B	E	A	C	I	V	I	L	R	O	I
9	K	L	C	L	Q	F	M	C	O	R	T	Y	M	L
10	B	I	T	E	B	Z	O	R	Y	F	L	Q	M	E
11	V	C	I	O	Y	O	T	T	W	S	E	V	O	R
12	I	N	D	E	P	E	N	D	E	N	T	Y	C	O
13	N	Z	N	Q	A	O	U	Z	W	V	K	O	L	Q

1. potato famine _____

2. _____

3. _____

4. _____

5. _____

6. _____

7. _____

8. _____

9. _____

10. _____

11. _____

12. _____

4 And before that?

*Match the sentences below with **after** (2x), **as soon as, when** (2x), **where** .... Be careful. You may have to change the tenses or start with a sentence from part B first!*

	A		B

A

1. The Romans brought their culture to the British Isles.
2. The Anglo-Saxon peoples came to Britain.
3. William of Orange began to move Protestants to Ulster.
4. Nearly half the Irish population died during the potato famines in the 19th century.
5. There were two years of civil war in Ireland.
6. In 1968 the fight for civil rights became terribly violent.

B

a) Finally southern Ireland became independent.
b) William of Orange crushed a Catholic uprising in 1690.
c) Only Celts lived in the British Isles.
d) The Celts were pushed to the north and west.
e) British soldiers were brought to Ulster in 1968.
f) Many Irish people began to leave Ireland.

1. _____

2. _____

3. _____

4. _____

5. _____

6. _____

Belfast – a divided city

1 A typical mistake

Complete the conversation on the next page with the expressions below.

I imagine...

I can't believe that...   No, not really.

I wonder why...

Maybe it's because...   What about...?   I didn't realize that...

Well, you see...

I'm surprised that...

That's right.

Silke and Mrs Brady are on their way to Mrs Brady's car in the car park at Belfast Airport.

Mrs Brady: Did you have a good flight, Silke?

Silke: _____ I had a middle seat and so I couldn't see very much.

Mrs Brady: _____ we'll be able to get you a seat next to a window when you go back

home. But _____ some food, Silke? Aren't you hungry?

Silke: _____ I had a little snack on the plane. And I couldn't eat, anyway.

_____ I was so excited. I've never been on a plane

before. And everything went so fast! Three hours ago I was still in Berlin. _____

_____ I'm in Belfast right now.

They are standing on the right-hand side of Mrs Brady's car.

Mrs Brady: Er... Silke, _____ you are over here? You should get in on the

other side.

Silke: Of course, _____ The driver is on the right,

and I have to sit on the left.

Mrs Brady: _____ It's just the opposite side. _____

_____ all our visitors from the Continent make the same mistake!

2 What do the following mean?

In Belfast, Silke saw a lot of graffiti everywhere. But not all of them were political slogans, as you can see here.
Can you write down what they mean?

I love you.
_____
_____
_____
_____
_____

At home with the Bradys

1 Right or wrong?

Read the text on page 15 of your English book again and then decide whether the following statements are right (+) or wrong (−).

a) Mrs Brady said:
1. "I'm Irish and I'm from the Isle of Skye."
2. "Spring comes early to the west coast of Scotland."
3. "Gaelic and English are very similar languages."
4. "This summer my husband and I want to go to a conference about minority languages in a village on the North Wales coast."
5. "I spoke Gaelic at school but English at home."
6. "My husband and I met at Edinburgh University twenty-five years ago."
7. "My husband loves Scotland but he didn't want to work and live there."
b) Jean said:
1. "My father has been teaching Irish Gaelic ever since the school was opened."
2. "My mother teaches Irish Gaelic, too."
c) Silke asked:
1. "Is it mild on the west coast of Scotland in winter?"
2. "Are Irish Gaelic and Scottish Gaelic similar languages?"
3. "Jean, what subjects do your parents teach?"
4. "Where is the conference on minority languages? Will it be in Ireland?"
5. "Mrs Brady, when did you meet your husband?"
d) Mr Brady asked:
1. "Silke, don't you want to phone home tonight?"

Now write whether the sentences above are right or wrong. Use your exercise book.

Example: a) 1. right: – She said (told, mentioned, answered, explained, added) that…

    or: a) 1. wrong: – She said that…

        c) 1. right: – She asked (wanted to know, wondered) …

2 The first day in Belfast

1. Jean and Silke were late for school.
2. Jean didn't lock the front door when she and Silke left in the morning.
3. Silke crossed the road. She looked left first and then right.
4. Jean crossed the road when the lights were red.
5. Mr Brady spoke so fast that Silke could not understand him.
6. Silke looked into a plastic bag that was standing in the corner of a music shop.
7. Silke and Jean came home after dark.
8. Mr Brady left the radio on all day.
9. Mrs Brady forgot to buy the tickets for the pop concert at the Information Centre.

What did they say to each other?

1. Mrs Brady told Jean and Silke _____

_____

2. Mr Brady asked Jean _____

_____

3. Jean told _____

_____

4. Silke asked _____

_____

5. Silke asked _____

_____

6. Jean asked _____

_____

7. Mr Brady told _____

_____

8. Mrs Brady told her husband _____

_____

9. The girls asked _____

_____

 A school with a difference

1 A college in Belfast

Write about a college in Belfast and use the diagram below to help you. Use your exercise book.

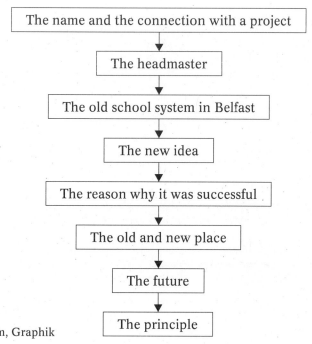

| The name and the connection with a project |
| ↓ |
| The headmaster |
| ↓ |
| The old school system in Belfast |
| ↓ |
| The new idea |
| ↓ |
| The reason why it was successful |
| ↓ |
| The old and new place |
| ↓ |
| The future |
| ↓ |
| The principle |

diagram [ˈdaɪəˌgræm] – Diagramm, Graphik

2 Lagan College

a) In the newsletter from Lagan College there were some sentences which read like an advertisement:

- Nobody must send their child to our college, but any child that wants to come to our school may come.
- You as parents and pupils should have faith in our project. It brings all the children together.
- Catholics need not be afraid of their Protestant neighbours and Protestants need not be afraid of their Catholic neighbours any more.
- Children can learn how to live in friendship with other religious groups.

What did the newsletter say? It said that ...

b) Here are Silke's reactions after her first day at Lagan College.

- "I could go to several different classes. The headmaster himself allowed me to do that."
- "I didn't have to say anything in the English course.
  I'm still unhappy about my German accent, you know."
- "I couldn't take part in the sports lesson because the teacher wouldn't let me into the gym with outdoor shoes."
- "I could understand most of the boys and girls although their accent was still new to me."
- "Unfortunately, I had to eat up all the food they gave me at lunch. I didn't like it much, but as a guest I couldn't really leave it, could I?"

Write down what you think Silke was (not) glad or happy about. Silke was glad that ...

Use your exercise book.

A phone call from Wales

1 The principle of the college

Fill in the 'K'. The letters in the squares 2 a, 8 d, 1 i, 3 g, 9 d, 16 a, 15 a, 12 a, 22 k, 21 b, 6 d, 17 g, give you the principle of Lagan College.

1. A group of people that does the same kind of work.
2. A large town in Ulster.
3. People who live in a country.
4. The civil rights problem is a ... problem.
5. A town or city with a long history can be called this.
6. Another word for land.
7. The capital of the Irish Republic.
8. Not noisy.
9. People who have a lot of money are ...
10. Neither.
11. Short form for United Kingdom.
12. The time before Christianity.
13. It is a Catholic organization in Ireland.
14. Potatoes grow in it.
15. Most important.
16. A religious holiday.
17. To see, to understand.
18. People eat them nearly everyday.
19. Adjective of religion.
20. In every place.
21. Meetings where people discuss things.
22. People live in their caravans there.

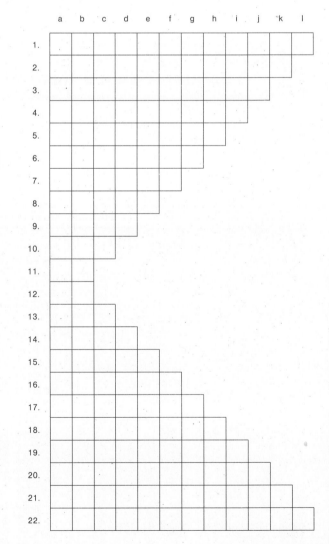

G There were roses

1 Word groups

Put the words below into five groups with four words in each group.

> song, bomb, soldier, Christian, people, happy, line, place, uprising, problem, war, Protestant, verse, positive, prison, sad, Catholic, negative, Moslem, chorus

1. religious groups _____ _____ _____ _____

2. disturbances _____ _____ _____ _____

3. feelings _____ _____ _____ _____

4. lyrics _____ _____ _____ _____

5. four P's _____ _____ _____ _____

⟨2 A telephone call⟩

Mache aus den folgenden Angaben zu einem Telefongespräch zuerst einen richtigen Dialog und übertrage ihn dann ins Englische.

Es klingelt bei Bradys. Ihre Telefonnummer ist Belfast 3 15 17.

Silke   Fiona

Sie meldet sich.

Sie meldet sich auch. Ist überrascht, daß Silke am Telefon ist. Sie wollte eigentlich Jean sprechen.

Sie sagt, daß Jean nicht da ist.

Sie fragt, ob sie weiß, wann sie wieder zurückkommt.

Sie hat leider keine Ahnung.
Sie fragt, ob sie etwas für Jean notieren kann.

Fiona bittet Silke, sie solle Jean fragen, ob Jean den Text von Chris de Burghs 'Don't pay the ferryman' habe. Sie sagt dann, daß Patrick ihr gestern erzählt habe, daß sie (Silke) sehr an irischer Volksmusik interessiert sei, daß ihr das Konzert vor ein paar Tagen sehr gut gefallen habe.

Silke bestätigt das.

Patrick habe ihr gestern auch gesagt, daß sie (Silke) schon bald wieder abreise.

Sie bedauert diese Tatsache, werde aber wiederkommen.

Sie hofft, daß Belfast dann eine (wieder) vereinigte Stadt ist. Sie sagt, daß man sich sicher vor ihrer Abreise noch einmal treffe und erinnert Silke daran, daß Jean zurückrufen solle.

Sie verspricht das.

Sie verabschiedet sich.

Sie verabschiedet sich ebenfalls.

UNIT 2

A The Big Apple

1 Places to see in New York City

2 Right or wrong?

If the statement is wrong, correct it in your exercise book.

1. New York City is the largest city in the U.S.A.
2. There are seven boroughs in New York and the most famous is Harlem.
3. About five and a half million people live in these boroughs.
4. The first immigrants who settled around New York were Dutch.
5. New York City was bought from the Indians for about twenty-four dollars.
6. You can see the Hudson River from the Statue of Liberty on Ellis Island.
7. There are more Irish immigrants who live in New York than there are Irish people who live in Ireland.
8. People who come from other towns and cities are called out-of-towners.
9. The subway is a type of car driven by a Guardian Angel.
10. The highest building in New York City has two towers.

A cab ride to Manhattan

1 Do you remember?

Read the text on page 31 of your English book. What did Gaetano say about the following? Write ten sentences (one for each picture) in your exercise book.

2 What would the other person say?

Look at what the Englishman or American woman says and write down what the other person would probably say. Use your exercise book.

"Crazy, man, crazy! Ya ain't gonna give that there cab driver 10 bucks!"

"Ain't ya gonna ask that cop the way to the Houses of Parliament?"

"Ya gonna be a dead duck if you walk down this street."

"I'm gonna take the subway to Buckingham Palace."

"I'm not going to take a taxi to Broadway, I'm going to walk."

"You certainly know your way around New York, Ed."

"You want to visit Macy's! That's great. I'm going to go with you."

13

C   I'd sure like to change a few things

1   An interview with a basketball player

a) This is one of the 500 interviews with New Yorkers.
   Make a list in your exercise book of:
   – all the things that have been said already and by whom;
   – all the ideas that are new.

b) *Rewrite the text in British English.*

"…What I'd most like to change in New York? Well, man, there are a number of important things. But first of all, I gotta say that there ain't no place on earth I'd rather be than in New York. I just love New York, man. Well, now to what I wanna see changed. Certainly the environment. We gotta have less pollution. That means safer public transport like the subway. People just gotta feel safe when they use it. Then, they gotta do something with the old houses – not just pull 'em down, man. Look what they done over there in the Bronx. They redeveloped whole streets and cheap, too. Do-it-yourself style. You know what I mean, man, everyone helps everyone. Education, yeah, that's a real problem, too. We gotta get the kids off the streets and give 'em a better education, 'specially in the poorer areas. …"

2   Other things New Yorkers say

Rewrite what these New Yorkers said in your exercise book.

Example: "It's difficult to get things to work here."
– Getting things to work here is difficult.

"It's fun to do things with young people and it keeps you young."

"It's as important today as ever to fight for your rights."

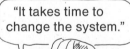
"It takes time to change the system."

"It's important to help to make changes yourself."

"It doesn't help just to watch."

"The easy way out is to wait for others to start."

3   Visitors to New York

Complete these sentences.

1. I (be afraid of – come) _____ here, but New York is just great for shopping.

2. Well, if you (interested in – see) _____ modern art like we are, New York is the place for you.

3. There's no (better reason for – visit) _____ New York than to see Manhattan's skyscrapers.

4. I've come here (in the hope of – find) _____ a coat in Macy's sale.

5. We (look forward to – come) _____ to New York to visit our children. They're all at college here.

6. Me? No, I'm not visiting New York. I'm (proud of – be) _____ a New Yorker myself.

7. This was a special offer, so we decided to take the (chance of – visit) _____

_____ New York before the prices go up again.

8. That's simple. We (feel like – go) _____ to a musical, and
there's no place like New York for that.

D   A refugee alone

1   Chanrithy

Use all the words in each line to make one sentence. Use your exercise book.

1. the Khmer Rouge / defeat / the government of Cambodia – *(want)*
2. the Khmer Rouge / kill / Chanrithy – *(try)*
3. one day / Chanrity / run away / from the camp – *(decide)*
4. he / take / his father / with him – *(plan)*
5. Chanrithy / go / to a Red Cross Camp / in Thailand – *(choose)*
6. he / learn / English / at the camp – *(begin)*

2   At the camp

Write down what Chanrithy and the Red Cross wanted / hoped / decided / expected / told…

Example: "Can you find my father?" – Chanrithy wanted the Red Cross to find his father.

1. _____

_____

2. _____

_____

3. _____

_____

4. _____

_____

5. _____

_____

15

Unit 2

3 A radio interview

The International High School has its own radio station. This is an interview with Chanrithy.
Use the information in brackets and complete the dialogue.

*****	****	***	**	*
love	enjoy	like mind prefer	can't stand	hate

IHS: "Hi, Chanrithy (*** – to tell) _____

_____ us where you were born?

Chanrithy: "I was born in Cambodia in 1971."

IHS: "You came to the U.S. to join your father in 1988, so you've lived here for a number of years now.

Can you tell us which country you (*** – to live) _____

_____ in?"

Chanrithy: "That's difficult because (I***** – to be) _____

_____ here in the U.S. You people are so kind. I (* – to think about) _____

_____ what happened to my father and me in

Cambodia, but when things get better, I think I (*** – to go back) _____."

IHS: "Perhaps you could tell us what you don't like here and what you think is better in Cambodia."

Chanrithy: "No, I don't think I can do that, but I can tell you what I find good here. I (**** – to receive)

_____ a good education and

being able to go to college. On the other hand, I (** – to think about) _____

the number of wars that are still going on everywhere. I (*** – to help) _____

make this a better world to live in – for everyone."

IHS: "Thank you, Chanrithy. Chanrithy is one of the many students who…"

E [The little guy]

1 Which language?

Put the verbs in brackets in their right forms.

1. When Chanrithy moved to the U.S. he (stop / use) _____ Cambodian

and just spoke American English.

2. At home he (try / speak) _____ Cambodian with his father but it was

very difficult.

3. It (mean / talk) _____ to his father in Cambodian and to everyone

   else in English.

4. When he went to college he (want / keep on) _____ talking and

   learning his mother language.

5. He (try / find) _____ some other Cambodians at or near the college,

   but there weren't any.

6. One day, he (stop / speak) _____ to a young girl who looked like she

   came from Cambodia. She did, but she couldn't speak the language very well.

7. She said she couldn't (remember / speak) _____ Cambodian since she

   came to the U.S.

8. She had heard that there was a group near the High School but she (forget / write down) _____

   _____ the address, so they decided to look for the group together.

9. They managed to find the group and (enjoy / practise) _____ their

   mother tongue until they both moved to different towns.

2 A helping hand

Read the story on page 38 of your English book again. Write one sentence for each picture to say what it has to do with the story.

Example:

1. _____

   _____

2. _____

   _____

3. _____

   _____

4. _____

   _____

5. _____

   _____

F I love New York

1 Say it in American English!

How would an *American* say or spell the following *British* words/expressions?

sweets
favourite
underground
centre
holiday
cinema
pavement
neighbour
flat
kilometre
someone from another town
garden
colour
harbour
lorry

2 True or false?

Some of these statements are false. Correct them in your exercise book.

1. 'Foreigners' give New York a bad name because they don't know what the city is really like.
2. You can't use the subway in New York on Sundays because it is too crowded.
3. Taxi drivers always take the shortest route from the airport to Manhattan.
4. Never argue with people in New York if they ask you for money, just give it to them.
5. In the rush hour it takes up to two hours to drive to the airport from downtown New York.
6. If your car breaks down on the East Side, they may kill you like a duck.
7. In all the restaurants in New York you must give the waiter $20 if you want to get a table.
8. Doctors in hospitals do not speak English on Sundays.

3 Negative expressions

Read 'I love New York' again. How many negative expressions can you remember or find?

1. _ _ m _ l _ _ _ _
2. b _ _ _ a _ e
3. _ _ n't _ r _ _ _ _
4. to g _ _ s _ _ _ o _ _
5. to _ _ _ _ k _ _ w _
6. to _ e _ t _ c k
7. B _ _ _ _ _ f _ _ !

8. to _ _ _ t s.o. _ p
9. to _ _ p _ f f s.th.
10. to _ _ t i _ t _ _ r _ u _ _ e
11. to k _ _ _ _ _ w _ y _ _ o _
12. to _ _ _ g _ u t
13. to _ _ t b _ _ _ _ n _ p
14. to k _ _ _ k s.th.

18

⟨4 New York⟩

Übersetze ins Englische.

Die Hauptstadt Amerikas ist nicht New York, sondern Washington. New York ist jedoch mit seinen 7 1/2 Millionen Einwohnern und fünf Stadtteilen die größte Stadt der USA. Die Einwanderung begann 1624. Vorher gehörte New York den Indianern, das ihnen für etwa $24 abgekauft wurde. Dort, wo Henry Hudson einmal landete, stehen heute viele der höchsten Gebäude der Welt. New York war ein großer Schmelztiegel der Nationen. Viele Kinder der Einwanderer haben nie ihr Heimatland und ihre Verwandten gesehen. Alle kamen, um ein neues Leben in einer neuen Welt zu beginnen.

UNIT 3

A Our national parks

1 Quiz time

Read pages 44 and 45 in your English book again and use a good map of the U.S.

1. In which state is the national park where you can ski down the longest slope in North America?
   (a) California   (b) Wyoming   (c) Idaho

2. Imagine you are in Salt Lake City. You want to go to a national park which is a deep narrow valley. Which direction do you have to drive?
   (a) west   (b) south   (c) north

3. Imagine you are in New York City. It is 12 o'clock and you are eating your lunch. Your friend, however, is in a national park with a lot of redwood trees. She is eating, too. What meal is she eating?
   (a) lunch   (b) evening meal   (c) breakfast

4. The first national park in the U.S. was created in
   (a) the 20th century (b) the 19th century (c) the 18th century

5. Why do posters in the Yellowstone National Park advise you to close your car windows? Because of
   (a) cold winds   (b) fires   (c) wild animals

6. In which state can you see a lot of trees which were there even before Jesus Christ was born?
   (a) California   (b) Tennessee   (c) Arizona

7. 'El Capitan' is
   (a) a waterfall in Yellowstone Park
   (b) a ski slope in Grand Teton Park
   (c) a rock face in Yosemite Park

8. America's population is about three times bigger than Germany's (about 80 million). The number of visitors to the national parks in a year is
   (a) smaller than   (b) bigger than   (c) as big as the population of the U.S.

2 National parks and national forests

Complete the text below with the verbs on the right. Use the correct tenses in the passive voice.

Two hundred years ago people in America did not think that nature would be destroyed

when trees **were cut down,** _____

when land _____
    for farms,

when 'improvements' _____
    to it by farmers,

when houses _____

and cities _____

to cut down
to take
to make
to build
to create

As modern life, however, threatened to damage nature

a law _____
    in 1864 to protect the most beautiful areas.

Since then, 49 parks _____

in which nature _____
    as it was before people arrived.

Since the early days of the national parks

wildlife _____ from people

and the landscape in them _____

to pass
to create
to keep
to protect
to change

To protect the national parks and the national forests

strict rules _____

Dogs cannot _____,

open fires must not _____,

and trash has to _____

to agree on
to take
to start
to collect

In spite of all these rules the national parks are very popular.
Over 300 million people visit them every year.

B The ski center

1 A lot of 'ifs' and 'buts'

Frank Mayer's ideas of a ski village were not welcomed by the residents of North Falls at first. Here is what people said to him:
1. "Draw up new plans and some of us will think differently."
2. "The whole thing should be examined by environmentalists. Then it can be discussed in a meeting with all the residents."
3. "If you can offer us jobs, some of us might say Yes to your plans."
4. "Offer good prices for our farms first. If you don't, we're not prepared to discuss your ski village."
5. "Nobody will accept your idea if you don't make plans to protect wildlife."
6. "Discuss your project with the state authorities* first. Then talk to us again."
7. "Give us all the facts. We must show them before we can discuss the pros and cons."

         authorities [ɔːˈθɒrətɪz] – Behörden

After a year, however, things were different. Some changes had been made because Frank Mayer did what people had told him to do.

Use the passive voice and complete the following sentences.

1. After _new plans had been drawn up,_ _____

   some people thought differently.

2. The whole thing was discussed in a meeting with all the residents because it _____

   _____

3. After jobs _____
   some of them said Yes to his plans.

4. They were prepared to discuss his ski village only when _____

   _____

5. Some people accepted his idea of a ski village because _____

   _____

6. After _____
   he talked to them again.

7. As soon as _____
   they discussed the pros and cons.

2 Frank Mayer's project

At the meeting in North Falls the local residents are still worried about Mr Mayer's project. They would like to have more information about

1. the damage to the environment
2. the protection of wildlife
3. the changes in their quality of life
4. the employment of local residents
5. the offer of a lot of service jobs
6. the improvement of local traffic
7. the creation of modern shops
8. the pollution of their valley
9. the destruction of the landscape

to create
to protect
to improve
to employ
to pollute
to change
to damage
to offer
to destroy

What do the local residents want to know?

1. They want to know _if the environment will be damaged._

2. They wonder if wildlife _____

3. They would like to know _____

   _____

4. They ask _____

5. They _____

_____

6. _____

_____

7. _____

_____

8. _____

_____

9. _____

_____

3 Different ways

Example:

1. At the meeting in North Falls Mr Mayer is showing the residents the plans.
   Example: At the meeting in North Falls Mr Mayer is showing the plans to the residents.
      or: At the meeting in North Falls the residents are being shown the plans by Mr Mayer.
      or: At the meeting in North Falls the plans are being shown to the residents by Mr Mayer.

2. Mr Mayer and his assistants are telling them all the facts.
3. Mr Mayer thinks that he can give work to everybody during the skiing season.
4. He says that even in summer a lot of jobs will be offered to the residents by his company.

Change the other sentences as many times as you can. Do this in your exercise book.

C The Grand Canyon

1 Problems in a national park

When some ViPs in the Grand Canyon National Park were asked about the problems, they said:

1. "People don't read our leaflets and so they don't take enough food along with them."

2. "…they don't even take a gallon of water per person because they don't pay attention to our warnings."

3. "As they don't wear good clothes, they get terribly cold when the weather changes."
4. "Many visitors to the park leave their bags with food on the ground overnight because they don't know anything about wild animals."
5. "Some even feed the animals with sweets and kill them."

6. "People don't use good maps because they don't believe the Canyon is a wilderness."
7. "They also damage the plants because they don't stay on the trails."
8. "We, the ViPs, have to collect their trash. Some people just leave it where they stay overnight."

How could things be made better for both tourists and ViPs?

1. If people read their leaflets, enough food _would be taken along._

2. A gallon of water _____

   if people _____

3. People _____

   if good clothes _____

4. Bags of food _____

   if many visitors _____

5. If animals _____

   they _____

6. If people _____

   good maps _____

7. Plants _____

   if people _____

8. If trash _____

   it _____

2 Preparing a trip in the Grand Canyon National Park

Summer time. Bob (American, 16) and Michael (German, 17) are staying at Grand Canyon Village.
They are making plans for the next few days.
Complete their conversation with the
expressions below.

but tell me   you are right   let's

that's a good idea   not really   how about?

I can't believe that   of course

I'd love   I imagine   no problem

you see   could you tell me?

Bob: _____ going right down to the river tomorrow?
            We could go as far as Trailview Overlook and then take the trail down.

Michael: _____ _____
            to do that. It'll be much more interesting than just walking along the Rim.

            _____ do you think we'll be able to do the trip in one day?

Bob: Hm, _____ _____,
from here it'll take us about an hour and a half to the point from where we can go down. Another three hours down to the river – and then back home again! How many hours is that then?

Michael: About 12 hours _____ We can't do that in a day.
We'll have to stay overnight. That means a heavy backpack.

Bob: _____, it does. First of all: Two gallons of water.

Michael: So much? _____
Do you want to have a shower or what?

Bob: No, of course not. But you need one gallon a day per person. And there are no stores, so …

Michael: …we'll have to take our food with us. At least we'll have something to eat then.

And _____ that our sleeping bags must be put in, too, because it will certainly be too cold and too hard without them at night. … What else?

Bob: Well, the guide says it can be very cold in a storm.

So _____ take our jackets, too.

Michael: _____ what your guide says about finding our way?

Bob: _____ for us. I've got a good map. It was the first thing
I bought when we arrived here.

3 Repairing the old railroad station

When Elliot and his friends arrived in to Grand Canyon Village to work as volunteers on the railroad station, Mr Sissons talked about the things that needed to be done. He said:

"Well, two good things first. The sheriff said we could leave the trash behind the station for a while and Mr Terson – he owns the garage over there – is letting us use one of his tractors. There's quite a bit of work, however, which has to be done immediately. You'll understand what I mean when you have a look at the place. See that tree over there? It's growing into the station. We really should cut it down. That window there has been broken for years. Do you think you can put a new one in? If you go inside you will see that water is coming through the roof. So that's another job for us. We've got to repair it. And I don't like the chimney stack. I think it's loose and might come down any time. How about taking it down today? … Hey! You don't look happy. Of course, you don't have to love me, but if you give me a smile, I'll feel that you like me!"

1. What did the sheriff and Mr Terson allow?

The sheriff allowed the _____

Mr Terson allowed one of his tractors _____

2. What did Mr Sissons want to be done immediately?

_____

_____

_____

_____

3. What did (didn't) Mr Sissons want for himself?

_____

_____

D The California Dream

1 The ups and downs of California

Read the text on page 52 again and then complete the sentences.

1. The great dream that brought people to California was that _____

_____

_____

_____

2. At first everybody thought that California _____

_____

3. But things have changed. The number of people who live in California is going down. Everybody can see

that because _____

_____

4. Housing prices have gone up so much that _____

_____

5. New suburbs _____

_____

6. There are also 25 million cars which _____

_____

7. Even in downtown San Diego – where life is quite comfortable – there are _____

_____

8. Although the State Government of California tries to protect wildlife and the wilderness, they cannot do

very much because _____

_____

2 Fiona McDonald

Read through the text on page 52 of your English book again and then answer the questions.
Use your exercise book.

1. Is Fiona Irish?
2. What were her jobs in San Diego?
3. Why did she leave San Diego?
4. What was the place like which she moved to?
5. How much time did she spend on commuting and work when she was living in Temecula?
6. What did commuting and work mean in her private life?
7. Where is she living now?
8. What kind of work does she do there?
9. Why does she like the environmental side of this area?
10. How has life changed for her?

3 Fiona's husband

Here are some of Fiona's husband's comments on life in California:

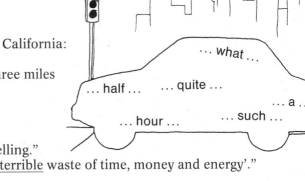

1. "By car it took me about <u>thirty minutes</u> to drive the three miles in downtown San Diego."
2. "House prices had become <u>a big</u> problem, too."
3. "I really couldn't stand <u>this kind of</u> life any more."
4. "Gas prices were OK. <u>One</u> gallon <u>for</u> $1.65."
5. "We sometimes spent eight hours <u>in one</u> day just travelling."
6. "I can only agree with Fiona when she said: '<u>This is a terrible</u> waste of time, money and energy'."

Express the underlined parts in a different way. Use the words on the right to help you.
Write the sentences in your exercise book.

E Vacation in the Grand Canyon

1 A weather forecast?

Write the first letter of the word under the number. All the letters form a sentence from a famous American pop song.

a) To shout in a high voice. --- 12, 15
b) To live out in the open air. --- 23
c) Everything you can see when you look at the countryside. --- 25
d) A person who does work for which he/she is not paid. --- 5
e) Injured. --- 19
f) If it is the only thing, it is ... --- 17
g) Peace and quiet. --- 2, 18

h) Chance to do what you like. --- 16, 28
i) Name of a famous rock face in a national park. --- 4, 6, 20
j) People live in them. --- 9, 24, 32
k) He/she looks after a national park. --- 7, 8, 21, 29
l) Not very wide. --- 3, 11, 14, 22, 30
m) You can see them when you walk in the snow. --- 27
n) To say something nasty to another person. --- 1, 10, 13, 26, 31

```
__ __    __ __ __ __ __    __ __ __ __ __    __ __    __ __ __ __ __ __ __ __
 1  2     3  4  5  6  7     8  9 10 11 12    13 14    15 16 17 18 19 20 21 22

__ __ __ __ __ __ __ __ __ __
23 24 25 26 27 28 29 30 31 32
```

2 Dangers in a national park

Active or passive voice? *Use the correct tense of the verbs in brackets.*

> ### GIRLS ELEVEN DAYS IN SNOW – GRAND TETON NIGHTMARE
>
> Lynn Barker and Jenny Gelmetti (have to stay) _____*had to stay*_____ in their caravan
>
> for eleven days when it (break down) _____ in snow on a mountain
>
> road. The only things the girls (can) _____ eat and drink were bread and water made
>
> from snow. During their long wait in the bitter cold they (play) _____ cards and (sing)
>
> _____ songs.

The teenagers (come back) _____ from a skiing holiday when they (lose) _____ their way 11,000 feet up in the mountains. The road (close) _____ but their car (find) _____ by two men who (ride) _____ snowmobiles*. "We (see) _____ the roof of a red car and when we (get) _____ closer, we (find) _____ the two girls. They (cry) _____ and (laugh) _____ at the same time. They (ask) _____ why nobody (look for) _____ them. The girls (say) _____ that they (start) _____ to walk, but the snow (be) _____ too deep for them. So they (decide) _____ to go back to their car. After their discovery, both girls (take) _____ to St Mary's Hospital in Idaho Falls. Dr Long, the hospital doctor, said: "They (do) _____ well. Just now they (take) _____ a hot bath as they _____ (be) so cold."

snowmobile ['snəʊməˌbiːl] – Schneemobil

Travels with Charley

1 Out in Yellowstone with Charley

Read pages 56 and 57 in your English book again and then complete the sentences.

1. When the narrator was near Yellowstone he

   _____
   because he was afraid of his neighbours' questions and comments.

2. Because he learned something new about his dog Charley,

   he _____

3. Dogs _____
   because of the bears, but the narrator kept Charley in his cab.

4. Bears are quite dangerous. They _____
   but they also get very angry with anybody who tries to tell them what to do.

5. When Charley saw his first bear, he _____

6. Charley _____
   and yet he acted as if he wanted to kill it.

7. The road _____
   as there were so many bears around.

8. The narrator _____

   _____ because of all the noise that Charley was making.

9. Later, in a restaurant, Charley _____
   while the narrator was having a drink.

10. Even the following night Charley _____

   _____ while he was asleep.

2 Dogs and bears   *How did John Steinbeck express the following?*

1. This dog is very friendly and quiet.

   _____

   _____

2. Charley will be so quiet that the bears won't even notice him.

   _____

   _____

3. The bears are terribly unfriendly.

   _____

   _____

4. The bears do not like people who get in their way.

   _____

   _____

5. Bears attack without warning.

   _____

6. Charley barked wildly at the bear.

   _____

7. The bear stood up.

   _____

8. There were quite a lot of bears.

   _____

9. Charley looks as if he could kill bears.

   _____

⟨3 In the restaurant⟩

Übertrage die ‚Gedanken' von John und Charley im Restaurant nach dem Besuch des Yellowstone Parks ins Englische.

Charley:

1. Was für ein komischer Park! Bären laufen frei herum und Hunde werden ins Auto gesteckt.
2. Man sollte den Bären mehr zum Fressen geben. Dann wären sie sicher netter.
3. Ich frag' mich, ob John wollte, daß die Bären mich fressen. Am Anfang war doch das (Wagen)fenster offen.
4. Ich mag' John nicht mehr. Er ist schon ein (ziemlicher) Feigling. Hat mir nicht mal gegen die schwarzen Hundemörder geholfen.

John:

1. Nächstes Mal wird Charley zu Hause gelassen.
2. Ich glaub', Reisen ohne ihn ist besser als eine halbe Stunde sein Bellen hören zu müssen.
3. Vielleicht würde man Hunde anders behandeln, wenn man ihre Sprache verstehen würde?
4. Der hintere Teil des Wagens sieht schrecklich aus. Ich kann's (fast) nicht glauben. Man wird ihn reinigen müssen. Wie wär's mit Charley?

UNIT 4

A Problems, problems!

1 Right or wrong?

Can you remember the text on pages 60 and 61 of your English book? Some of the following statements are wrong. Find them and correct them in your exercise book.

1. Every week the Russell Sixth Form College Radio Station broadcasts a programme about youth problems.
2. This radio station broadcasts more than six times a week.
3. As far as the text is concerned, an adult is someone who can look after himself or herself.
4. There is a postbox in the school hall for pupils' comments and ideas.
5. 27% of the people interviewed in the National Youth Survey said they could go to X movies.
6. Over 400 said that they have to tell their parents where they are going before they can go out.
7. Most parents in the survey didn't tell their children when they had to be home.
8. Some of those asked thought that they were already adult at the age of twelve.

2 Problems at the police station

A number of people offer to help the police because they saw what happened.
Make <u>one</u> sentence out of the two and add a relative pronoun.

1. That is definitely the man. He broke into the bank yesterday.

_____

_____

2. I recognize the young man. He was driving the car.

_____

_____

3. I am sure she is the woman. She was in the bank, too.

_____

_____

4. That is the lorry. It was parked round the corner.

_____

_____

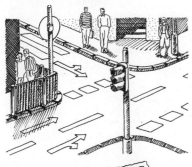

5. Yes, I recognize the place. The accident happened here.

_____

_____

6. These are the photos. They were taken during the robbery.

_____

_____

3 Problems!

Rewrite the sentences in your exercise book. Leave out the <u>relative pronoun</u> where possible. Be careful about the position of the preposition.

1. This is a photo of the boy about whom we have just been talking.
2. I met him at the disco which I went to with my sister last week.
3. He's the boy with whom my sister danced all evening.
4. Do you remember? He's the one to whose party she is going this evening.
5. Hasn't he got a sister for whom Mary did some babysitting?
6. Yes, and a huge dog with which he often goes for a walk near our school.
7. Ah, now I know about whom you are talking.
8. He's the boy with whom I have been going out for months. I wonder where your sister is now!

4 Jenny's fax

Jenny sent this fax to her penfriend in New York.

Dear Kathy,

It's a crazy world. Do you remember that g . . . . . . been going out w . . . ? Well, he has just told m . . . . . .

coming to New York. The comp . . . . he work . . . . . . decided to send him there for six weeks. Can you

look for a plac . . . . can stay? He will get some extra money – about $500 – . . . . he will be able to

pay the rent, etc. Will that be enough?

I'm sur . . . . . . will have enough time to show him all the sights. And don't forget to take him to the new

shopping cent . . . . showed me. I don't kno . . . . ght he will be taking but as soon as I do, I'll fax

the details to you. Hope you will fax back soon.

Love,

Jenny

PS: Here is a copy of his photo. I hope that it will be clear when it comes through on your fax.

The fax arrived, but some of the letter could not be read. *Write the letter in your exercise book. Fill in the missing parts.*

 ## Double trouble

1 Which goes with which?

Put the sentences together to make one and write them in your exercise book. Use a relative pronoun and don't forget the commas. You may need to read the text on pages 63 and 64 of your English book again.

For example: The Russell Band, which went to Germany on a tour this summer, gets its name from a college in England.

The Russell Band gets its name from a college in England.

During the tour the group gave concerts in a number of cities.

In Aachen, they gave a concert at a school.

Phil played the saxophone in the band.

Katy sent a letter for the school notice-board.

The other orchestra took the double bass with them by mistake.

Manuela's father took Katy back to his house for a barbecue.

Münster was the next town on the band's tour.

Manuela's father borrowed a truck from a neighbour.

Katy's double bass was 'stolen' at the railway station.

The other orchestra left the station in a truck.

Münster also has a youth hostel.

Katy thought Aachen was a super place.

The tour lasted for about a week.

Phil broke his arm in Germany.

The band went to Germany on a tour this summer.

31

2 An evening out with Thomas

Put the two sentences together to make one sentence. Be careful! Sometimes you need a relative pronoun, and sometimes you also need commas. Write the sentences in your exercise book.

1. Katy and Manuela took Thomas out for the evening. Thomas had taken Katy's double bass by mistake.
2. First, they went to a youth club. Manuela goes to the youth club every week.
3. There they played table-tennis and ate some food. The club leader always cooked for the members.
4. Later, they decided to join some of Manuela's friends. The friends were going to a disco on the other side of town.
5. Katy had never been to a German disco before. Katy loved dancing.
6. Thomas spent the rest of the evening dancing with the girls. Thomas was the only boy in the group.
7. At twelve o'clock they phoned Manuela's father. Manuela's father picked them up and took them home.
8. Katy, Manuela and Thomas had a wonderful evening. They still write to each other.

[3 Phil's arm]

Rewrite the sentences in your exercise book. Use an adverbial clause for the participle constructions that are underlined.

1. <u>Having finished</u> his work for the concert, Phil decided to go into town.
2. <u>Having reached</u> the main shopping centre, Phil went into a shop to look for presents.
3. <u>While looking at</u> some postcards, he saw an accident outside the shop.
4. <u>Running out of</u> the shop to help, he forgot to look left.
5. <u>Crossing</u> the road to get to the injured person, he was hit by a young man on a bike.
6. <u>Trying</u> to get up, he realized that his arm was broken.
7. <u>Not knowing</u> what to do, he asked someone for help.
8. <u>Having arrived</u> at the hospital, he was soon looked after by a doctor.

American Football

1 Who's who?

Can you remember something about each of these people? If not, read the text on pages 66 and 67 of your English book again. Write one or two sentences about each person in your exercise book.

Example: Sam Lee is someone who has a radio programme called 'Letter from the U.S.A.'.

Now go on.

2 All in a game of football

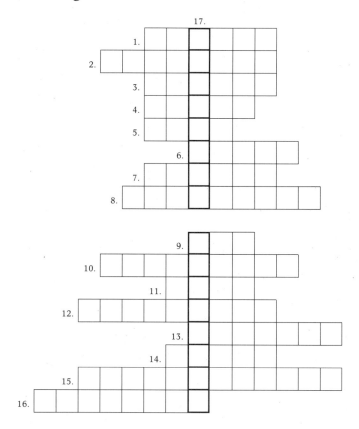

ACROSS:

1. Time of year when this game is played.
2. Someone who believes the best will happen.
3. Someone who looks very nice.
4. Angry word(s) which someone says.
5. A large smile on someone's face.
6. To say, sing or shout together.
7. A number of teams which play against each other.
8. Not known to anyone.
9. Some people say jogging keeps you …
10. At many American colleges sports are very important, so the teams take their game …
11. Everyone drinks this in the U.S.A.
12. To tell people about something by putting it in the newspaper.
13. To take in air.
14. To move to music.
15. Girls who shout for a team at a game.
16. Of a nation or state.

DOWN:

17. _____

 What's wrong?

1 Missing words?

Complete the text. Put in the missing words in the right places. Add a relative pronoun if necessary.

Mary: I've tried _____ I can think of to get better marks.

Chris: Is there _____ I can do to help you, Mary?

Mary: Well, _____ we can do, I suppose, is to stop seeing each other so often.

Chris: That was _____ I was going to talk to you about anyway, Mary. My marks have been pretty bad, too, in the last few weeks.

Mary: I told my Mum you are _____ really understands me.

Chris: Well, I try. There is _____ still worries me, though.

Mary: Really! I thought that there was _____ worried you!

Chris: Ha, ha! Do you think that is _____ your parents will expect us to do? I know they don't like me very much.

Mary: _____ I can say is that they might stop us from going to the ice hockey together.

Chris: I don't think so. There's _____ would stop your parents from going, so we could just go with them!

2 Language differences

Here are parts of two dialogues. *Use the sentences on the right to complete the dialogues.*
Write them in your exercise book.

Dialogue A:

Mum: I know why you always come home late, Cindy. . . .
Cindy: No, it's not. Tom's all right! . . .
Mum: What do you mean – not early enough! You're not eighteen yet. . . .
Cindy: Leave me alone, will you! . . .

Dialogue B:

Mum: I'm a little worried, Cindy. . . .
Cindy: I know, Mum. I feel really tired, too. . . .
Mum: You probably need more sleep, then. . . .
Cindy: No, you can't, Mum. It's up to me. . . .

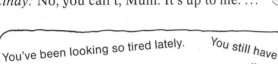

You've been looking so tired lately.   You still have to do what I tell you.   I'll make sure I'm in on time in future, I promise.

I'll have to do something about it.

I could never come home early enough for you.   Can I help you in any way?   It's that friend of yours, Tom.

I know what is good for me and what is not.

The cool chick

1 Getting it right

Can you complete the sentences? Write them in your exercise book.

1. When Marco asked Isabel to go to the party
   a) she wasn't at all surprised.
   b) she was feeling rather cold.
   c) she wanted to ask her parents first.
   d) she thought it was a trick.

2. Her parents didn't want her to go out with Marco because
   a) they didn't trust them.
   b) he was older than she was.
   c) they wanted to stop boys asking her out.
   d) they had found out how much she wanted to go.

3. The party took place in a house
   a) which was empty.
   b) which was owned by Marco's parents.
   c) where the football team met regularly.
   d) John Wintersize said they could use.

4. Isabel's parents wanted
   a) her to be back home by a quarter past one.
   b) Marco to bring Isabel home by one o'clock.
   c) her to return home if she didn't feel comfortable.
   d) to stop Marco from cradle-robbing.

5. When Marco didn't get up
   a) Izzy started to tell jokes.
   b) another boy offered to take her home.
   c) she knew he had been drinking too much.
   d) she offered him a cup of coffee.

6. When Izzy was sitting in the car
   a) she felt quite hot.
   b) she thought VW bugs always went fast.
   c) she thought about what her parents would say.
   d) all she could think of was getting home.

7. The last thing Izzy remembered before the accident was that
   a) Marco said he was going too fast.
   b) she saw a tree which moved across the road.
   c) the car was going to hit a tree.
   d) Marco didn't stop at the stop sign.

8. The first thing Izzy remembered after the accident was
   a) that she had lost a leg.
   b) that she had a tree on top of her.
   c) when Dr Carstairs called her name.
   d) Marco's face.

2 A crossword puzzle

ACROSS:

1. A place to spend the night.
5. A place to go for a drink but you should be eighteen.
7. You think he did it.
12. Certainly not old.
14. Not me but the person I am talking to.
16. Places where ships go in a storm.
17. Not the beginning.
18. You may speak with a funny one.
20. For this reason.
21. One more than this.
25. He wrote Greek poems (H....).
27. Not to stay a long time.
28. Short form of 'professional'.
29. For example.
30. Not to be seen when it is cloudy or at night.
31. Yesterday, at dinner.
32. There are fifty of them in the U.S.A.
34. Number one.
35. Not a dream.
36. What you are hoping to do.
38. See if you can do it.
40. Friendly and kind.
43. As well.
45. Like.
46. No one knows, for example, who wrote it.
48. They are very comfortable to sit in.
51. Americans say this to everyone.
52. Indefinite article before a word like 'apple'.
53. A boy's name.
55. You're likely to be this when it rains.
57. For business.
60. There's no noise at all.

DOWN:

1. You eat it early in the morning.
2. Finding something for the first time.
3. It says where something is.
4. A word for myself.
6. A boy's name.
7. They have all the sides the same length and at 90°.
8. You call this in an emergency.
9. You see with it.
10. If you agree.
11. England at the time of Henry VIII.
13. The time to do something.
15. Not very often 'late'.
19. You need this if you want to smell something.
21. A place where.
22. Thinks everything will be good.
23. To travel a long way on foot.
24. Don't touch it or you may burn yourself.
26. It could be rock-'n-roll or jazz.
32. To tell someone something.
33. To take in food.
34. It could have been 'and' or 'because'.
37. To be successful in an exam.
39. He looks after the national parks.
40. Not a long time in the future.
41. A terrible battle against the Indians.
42. Short form of 'etcetera'.
43. 'Some' – but in questions.
44. Not large.
45. The size of a piece of land.
47. Not going in.
49. But not what you call your dad.
50. Not yours, mine or his.
54. The other part of it is 'cream'.
56. Opposite of 'out'.
58. Of me.
59. Short form for 'that is'.

⟨**3 A postcard to Sharon**⟩

Translate the postcard into English in your exercise book.

Hallo Sharon!

Hier eine (Ansichts)karte aus N.Y.,
die erste Station auf meiner Reise.
Sam, dessen Foto ich Dir gezeigt
habe, holte mich am Flughafen ab.
Erinnerst Du Dich, es ist der Junge,
der mir versprochen hat, Amerika
zu zeigen? Ich weiß nicht, welchen
Teil Amerikas wir sehen werden,
aber N.Y. ist großartig und ein
guter Anfang. Morgen gehen wir
nach New Orleans, wo Onkel Tom
in der Hütte gelebt hat.
Ich werde Dir von dort eine Karte
schreiben. *Ben*

Sharon Smith

24 Martin Street

Southampton

Hampshire SO63 6BW

UK

UNIT 5

 ## A The Industrial Revolution

> Nikolaus Otto
> Christopher Columbus
> Henry Bessemer
> Captain Cook
> Louis Daguerre John Cabot
> Otto von Goericke Alexander Graham Bell
> Johann Gutenberg
> George Stevenson

1 Discoverers and inventors

Who discovered, invented, or built the first…? *Find the right people
and use 'to discover' (3×), 'to invent' (6×) and 'to build' (2×).*

1. Christopher Columbus discovered America.

2. _____ a method of taking photographs.

3. _____ a method of producing steel from iron.

4. _____ the petrol engine.

5. _____ Australia.

6. _____ the telephone.

7. _____ the printing press.

8. _____ the air pump.

9. _____ Newfoundland on 24th July 1497.

10. _____ the first steam passenger railway.

11. _____ the first steam engines which could be used in factories.

2 Another big development

The development of coal gas during the Industrial Revolution brought many advantages to the people.
Some of them are explained here. *Make complete sentences and write them in your exercise book.*

1. in Britain / to make / coal gas / first in 1727
2. as a light / George Dixon / to use / about thirty years later, / the gas / in his house / for the first time
3. than the light / to be / much better / the gas light / from oil lamps
4. in closed ovens* / to make / coal gas / by heating coal
5. but Dixon and other British experts / to be / the process / safe ways of producing it / to find / in lights / and then using it / rather dangerous
6. people's lives / to change / in a lot / gas lighting / of ways
7. cities / safer places / with street lighting / to become
8. in factories, / which / to mean / that / goods / to use / too, / at night / they / could produce / it
9. at night schools / to allow / gas lighting / also / to learn / people / after work
10. coal gas / later / to use / homes / in the nineteenth century, / for heating
11. more comfort / who / could afford / less work / them / to mean / gas fires / for those / and / to be

* *oven* ['ʌvn] – Ofen

B   The good old days?

1 Life and work during the Industrial Revolution

Rebecca, one of the schoolgirls at Wallsend Comprehensive School, had to write a report for a project on the Industrial Revolution in Britain. Here are her notes.

> 1. Transport:
>   a) Travelling long distances was very hard.
>   b) Going by stage coach was too expensive for poor people.
> 2. The mines:
>   c) In the first half of the eighteenth century the iron industry wanted to get more coal for their iron production. It was really necessary for them (Machines were made of iron!!)
>   d) But the mines were not deep enough and so they couldn't provide all the coal needed by the iron industry.
>   e) When the workers went down deeper, they couldn't work there. There was too much water.
>   f) The new steam engine was simple but it was good enough for one thing. It could pump the water out of the mines.
> 3. Waste and the iron and coal industry:
>   g) Putting the slag back into the mines was too expensive and too slow.
>   h) Building the slag heaps next to the mines seemed to be easy enough...
>   i) ... but living next to slag heaps became very dangerous for the workers.
> 4. Quality of life:
>   j) Children couldn't play in the streets or go to school. With all the work there were simply no time.
>   k) Poor people couldn't improve their lives in the slums. There were just no chances for them.

Rewrite the notes and use infinitive constructions. You may shorten statements and join sentences. Start like this:
a) It was hard to...
b) It was too expensive for poor people...
c) In the first half of the eighteenth century it was necessary...   *Do this in your exercise book.*

2 Newcomen's steam engine (1712)

Mr Fry, a teacher at Rebecca's school, was talking to Rebecca's class about his idea for the project on the Industrial Revolution.

a) The model pump

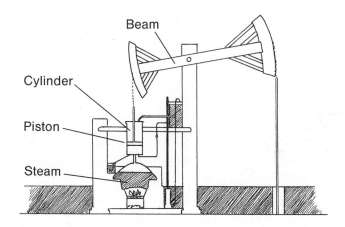

"While I was looking for drawings **which could describe** some old machines, I found this one here. It's a drawing of Newcomen's invention. It was the first steam engine **which worked** in Britain and it was used as a water pump. In fact, in the early 18th century the steam pump was the only machine **which pumped** the water out of the mines... fast, cheaply and twenty-four hours a day, I mean.

Do you think the drawing is good enough to show us a way **in which we can build** a small model pump here in the workshop? I'm sure the fastest team **which produces** a model that works will get a prize from the headmaster."

Shorten Mr Fry's sentences with infinitives whenever it is possible. Write the sentences in your exercise book.

b) Problems to solve

1. Who should we choose as captains of our teams?
2. What materials should we use?
3. Should we use wood or steel for the beam?
4. How can we link the piston to the beam?
5. Which methods could we use to produce steam?
6. What size should the cylinder be?
7. Should we heat the water with oil, coal or gas?
8. What can we do about our 'little' waste problems?

The pupils asked themselves...

Example: 1. ___who to choose as captains of their teams.___

 Choosing a career

1 Ifs and buts...

Read the text on page 84 of your English book again and then finish the sentences.

1. The boys and girls of Form 5C at Wallsend Comprehensive School were in their final year at school but

   they _____

   _____

2. Even if the pupils wanted to go on to a Sixth Form College, they _____

_____

_____

3. For Wendy Long and her classmates the problem was quite clear: They could only take A-levels at a Sixth

Form College if they _____

_____

4. Mrs Johnson's advice to Wendy was: Unless _____

_____ you won't pass and if you don't get good enough grades in your other five subjects, you

_____

5. Rick Brown, her boyfriend, had no problems in his eight subjects, but his father _____

_____

6. Rick, however, thought that he would have better chances of getting a good job if he _____

_____

7. He had not given up dreaming: If he could only convince his father with the help of the Careers Teacher

that it would be better to stay on at school, his father _____

8. The Careers Teacher's advice to Wendy Long was very clear: If _____

_____

have a look at the Jobcentre's brochure, and if you find an interesting job, _____

_____

2 Wendy's plan

Wendy is sure that she will be able to solve her school problems. Here is her plan:

> No more discos...   then...   more time for homework...   then
>
> ...improvement in my school marks   ...then   ...good exam grades in seven subjects...
>
> then...   place at Sixth Form College...   then...   same class as Rick...   then...
>
> see him more often at school...   then...   no more discos...   then...

Write down what will happen if she can keep to her plan. Use your exercise book.
Start like this: If she doesn't go to discos any more, she will have...

3 Rick Brown

Here is what his parents, teachers and classmates say about him:

1. He works hard for school.

3. He is not interested in cars.

2. He does not go out very often.

4. He really wants to stay on at school.

6. He wants a career in international banking.

5. He is not keen on a career in the car business.

7. He prefers academic subjects to practical subjects.

What do think would happen if Rick Brown had a different attitude to his work or if he preferred other things? *Write the answers in your exercise book. Start sentences 1, 3, 5, 7 with the main clause, the other sentences with the if-clause.*

 Applying for a holiday job

1 The wrong reply!

The Rochdale Observer, 4th April 1993

Are you looking for a holiday adventure abroad? Can you understand and speak French? Do you like children and household work? Then spend July/August with us in southern France. English family (2 adults, 2 children – boy, 5 and girl, 3) need au-pair to help them in their holiday home. We offer own room and generous pocket money. Girls with driving licence contact Mrs Simmons, 20 Margaret Avenue, Rochdale, Lancs. Applications must include CVs and refs.

Pamela Wiggins wrote to Mrs Simmons. When she was out of her room, her sister Peggy changed some of the words on the computer screen. *Put the letter back into its old form, making changes to style and vocabulary.*

15 King Street
Rochdale, Lancs
RO2 6BD
1st April 1993

Hello Mrs Simmons,
I saw your ad in yesterday's Rochdale Observer. You are offering a job as an au-pair this winter and I would like to apply for it.
I think I have all the qualities needed for this kind of work. I have done five days of Welsh and am convinced that I have no problems in understanding or speaking it. During the last two years I have worked at our local ANIMALS' HOME and looked after some of the animals regularly. It gave me a lot of pleasure and so I think I could have a lot of fun together with your animals. Your household work should not be any problem at all, because my mother says that I am really not good at it.
I had to have a dog licence while working at the ANIMALS' HOME because I had to use my parents' car to get there quickly.

Bye for now.
Love,

2 Mister X

Write Mr X's CV in your exercise book.

- He has got the same first name as Columbus, the discoverer of America.
- His family name has two parts: The first is the opposite of 'big' or 'great', the second is the material you get from trees.
- He lives in the city near which the first steam engine was used to pump water out of the coal mines.
- The street where he lives was named after Queen Elizabeth's father.
- The number of his house is the same as the day of the month when John Cabot landed north of Newfoundland in 1497.
- He was born on the day when summer starts.
- You can easily find out the year of his birth: he passed his driving test as early as possible and will get his driving licence on his birthday this year.
- He was born in the Welsh capital.
- His father Peter worked in a coal mine but he lost his job three months ago. At the moment he has no work.
- His mother Patricia sells goods in a big shop.
- His school career: First he was at St Patrick's in the Welsh capital. From the age of nine he went for six years to a comprehensive school in Lagan, a suburb of the northern Irish capital. At present he is at the Brabham Sixth Form College in the city where he lives with his parents.
- He would like to go on to university and work as somebody who teaches foreign languages.

Two replies

1 Things would have been different if...

1. Wendy included all the necessary information in her letter of application and so Mr Watson wrote back to her.

If Wendy had not included all the necessary information in her letter of application, Mr Watson would not have written back to her.

2. It took Mr Watson a long time to reply to all the letters because he had such a lot of applications.

   If Mr Watson _____

   _____

   _____

3. Some young people were not old enough and so they could not be considered for the jobs.

   Some young people _____

   _____

   _____

4. Wendy had already been at a GTH camp. This was the reason why Mr Watson asked her for an interview.

   If Wendy _____

   _____

   _____

5. Mr Watson was planning to interview Wendy in York because there were so many applications from the north of England.

   Mr Watson _____

   _____

   _____

6. Wendy's friend Linda could not apply for a GTH job because she had promised to work in her mother's café.

   If Wendy's friend Linda _____

   _____

   _____

7. Linda's boyfriend had moved to Australia, which made her a little sad.

   Linda _____

   _____

   _____

8. Linda did not know that Wendy was looking for a holiday job and so she did not ask her mother to find her one. If Linda _____

   _____

   _____

9. Linda's father had one reason why he did not have the telephone reconnected: She was not able to promise not to call Steve more than once a week. Linda's father _____

   _____

   _____

2 Wendy's phone call

Before agreeing to go to the interview with Mr Watson, Wendy decided to phone Mr Watson's agency to find out more about two important things. *Complete the dialogue with the expressions below.*

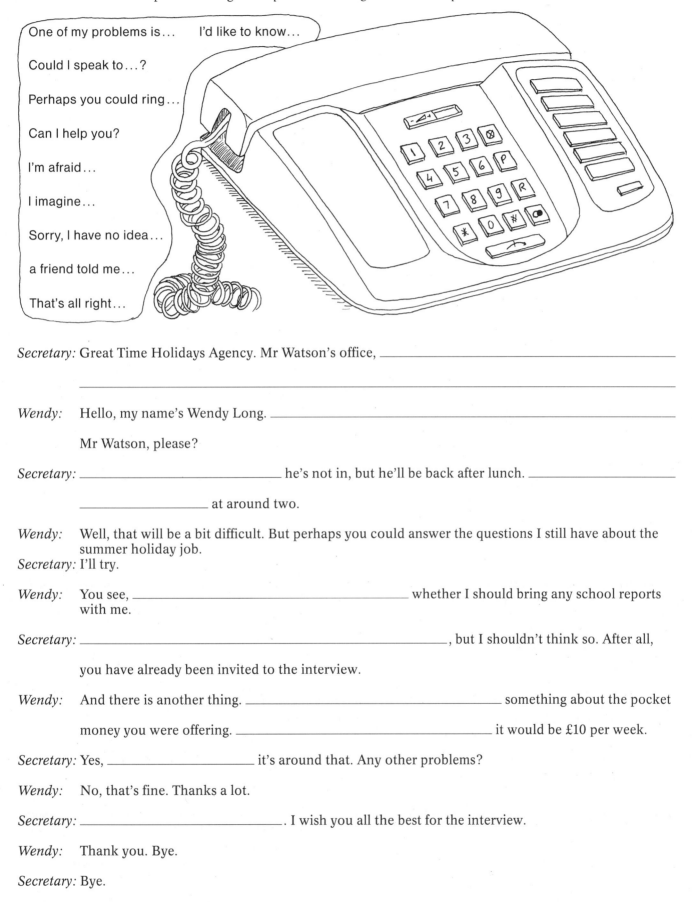

One of my problems is...   I'd like to know...

Could I speak to...?

Perhaps you could ring...

Can I help you?

I'm afraid...

I imagine...

Sorry, I have no idea...

a friend told me...

That's all right...

Secretary: Great Time Holidays Agency. Mr Watson's office, _____

_____

Wendy: Hello, my name's Wendy Long. _____

Mr Watson, please?

Secretary: _____ he's not in, but he'll be back after lunch. _____

_____ at around two.

Wendy: Well, that will be a bit difficult. But perhaps you could answer the questions I still have about the summer holiday job.

Secretary: I'll try.

Wendy: You see, _____ whether I should bring any school reports with me.

Secretary: _____, but I shouldn't think so. After all,

you have already been invited to the interview.

Wendy: And there is another thing. _____ something about the pocket

money you were offering. _____ it would be £10 per week.

Secretary: Yes, _____ it's around that. Any other problems?

Wendy: No, that's fine. Thanks a lot.

Secretary: _____. I wish you all the best for the interview.

Wendy: Thank you. Bye.

Secretary: Bye.

1 A puzzle

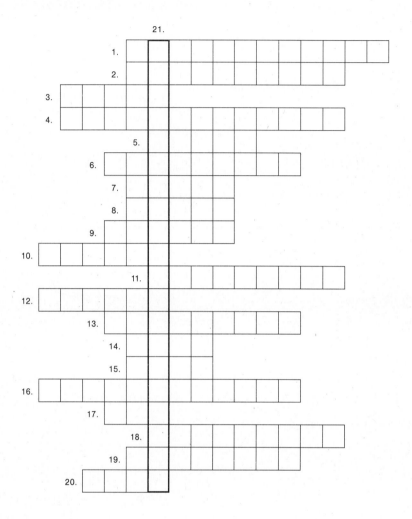

1. Opposite of advantage.
2. Without a job.
3. You can hear it.
4. A process of giving or broadcasting information to many people.
5. All the people who work for a firm.
6. Working with materials such as iron or steel.
7. Opposite of long.
8. Somebody who works in a mine.
9. A small church.
10. When a dead person is put in a grave it is a...
11. To link two things which had been together before but are not together now.
12. Cats like it when you do this.
13. Creating something new.
14. A young or a small horse.
15. The waste of mines or ironworks.
16. Everything that has to do with farms.
17. A mine.
18. Where iron is made.
19. Alone.
20. Wanting to do something very much.
21. An expression for a time when great changes in industry were made.

G **A day in the life of a coal miner**

1 Why?

Read the text on pages 92 and 93 of your English book again and write the answers in your exercise book.

1. Why can the old miner remember his first Monday at work so well?
2. Why did he not need an alarm clock that morning?
3. Why could his brother give him advice for his first day at work?
4. Why was advice about the safety lamp so important?
5. Why did the miner compare the lift to a cage?
6. Why was he tired at the end of the day?
7. Why did he feel sorry for the ponies that worked in the mines?
8. Why did he stay at home for two days after the Stanley disaster?
9. Why did he keep an old postcard which shows 30 miners?
10. Why were those first years in the mines happy days for him?
11. Why has he also got unhappy memories of his working life?

2 At the Working Men's Club

The old men at the Working Men's Club are comparing the old days with today. *Fill in the correct forms of* **to take, to have, to do,** *or* **to make.**

1. In those days people used to be fair. When someone had to ___*do*___ a difficult job, another

   worker _____ over after a while. We used to _____ turns, you know.

2. That's right. It was the same at our clubs. When we _____ a mess on the tables or damaged

   something, we cleaned it up or repaired it, or _____ somebody else _____ it for us.

   These young people today just walk away.

3. Or _____ a look at education. We _____ to pay for everything. It was a good thing,

   though. When you _____ a course, you tried to finish it and at the end you _____

   an exam. And today, when everything is free? If they don't like it, they drop it.

4. I don't think our children are so bad. In my daughter's family they share a lot of the work. My mother still

   _____ to _____ all the household work. In my daughter's family it's different. Her

   husband _____ the shopping, my grandchildren _____ the dishes and everybody

   _____ his own bed.

5. Or think of the meals. We _____ our packed lunches along to the factory. Today most people

   can _____ lunch in the canteen or cafeteria, as they call it.

⟨3 An ad⟩

Felix Kuntz
Ralf-Mayer-Weg 36
44575 Castrop-Rauxel 4

Mr Downie
Pleasure Cottage
Hill Drive, Crawley

Sussex

Castrop-Rauxel, den 21. Juli 1993

Sehr geehrter Herr Downie,

ich habe erst gestern Ihre Anzeige vom 6. Juli 1993 im Sussex Chronicle von einem englischen Freund erhalten. Deshalb schreibe ich Ihnen so spät, hoffe aber zugleich, daß es nicht zu spät ist. Ich bin 20 Jahre alt und studiere Englisch und Französisch an der Universität Bochum. Ich glaube, daß ich Ihnen bei der angebotenen Arbeit sehr gut nützen kann, da ich schon seit Jahren mein Taschengeld mit Gartenarbeit, die ich am Wochenende ausführe, verdiene.

Ich sollte vielleicht erwähnen, daß ich mich bei Ihnen auch dann beworben hätte, wenn Ihr Angebot weniger großzügig gewesen wäre. Wenn Sie mir die Gelegenheit geben würden, bei Ihnen zu arbeiten, würde ich Ihnen sicher auf vielfältige Weise helfen können. Beiliegend finden Sie einen kurzen Lebenslauf. Sollten Sie noch weitere Informationen benötigen, rufen Sie mich bitte abends unter 0 23 05 - 61 82 an.

In der Hoffnung auf eine baldige Antwort, verbleibe ich
mit freundlichen Grüßen

Felix Kuntz

Felix Kuntz aus Castrop-Rauxel hat die Anzeige von seinem englischen Freund Graham Tucker mit zwei Wochen Verspätung bekommen. Hier ist sein Briefentwurf:

Translate Felix's letter into English.

UNIT 6

A Sometimes progress costs the Earth

1 A new way to Britain

Can you find the right words to fit these definitions?

1. The open land outside of towns and cities.
2. A special place that families and children visit for fun.
3. Small, narrow river.
4. Road, usually very narrow, which you use to go from one village to the next.
5. Someone who is very interested in everything that is going on around him/her.
6. Row of small trees often planted between fields and along roads.
7. Animals and birds that live in the forests and fields around us.
8. A small animal with long ears which some people keep at home.
9. Things which a country, organization or person has which they can use e.g. coal.
10. Keep things as they are and not let them get worse e.g. an old house.

11. Small animal with six legs, many of which can fly.
12. Used to describe those animals of which there are not many left e.g. panda bears.
13. Life on a farm or in a village but not in a town, or city.

14. The new way to get to Britain is the ___ __ __ __ __ __ __   __ __ __ __ __ __ __

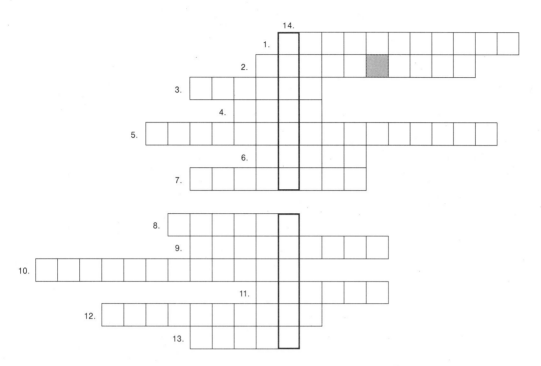

2 Why not?

You are at a meeting of a group of young people who are discussing 'The green country code'. Some of the young people are asking questions about the code.
Write down your answers to their questions.

3 Friends of the Earth

Imagine you are writing a letter to 'Friends of the Earth'. Tell them a little about yourself and what you are doing to protect the environment. Ask them for information about FoE groups near where you live and how to join.

4 Then and now

Can you describe the differences between the two pictures?
Why do you think these changes have taken place?
Would you prefer to live now or then? Give reasons.

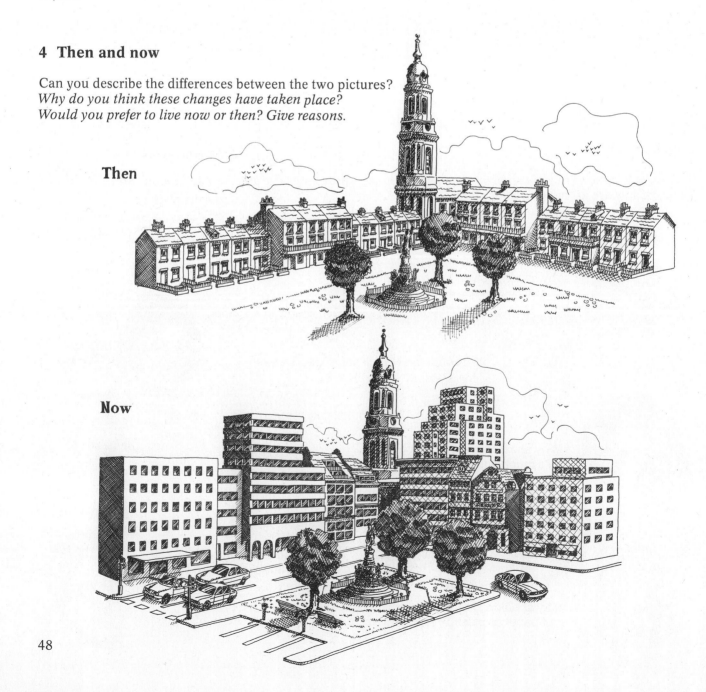

Then

Now

The deal

1 Questions on the text

1. Why do you think Mr Hunt was not looking very happy when he talked to the Canadians?
2. What do the Canadians want to do with Highams Hill Farm?
3. What reason does Mr Hunt give for selling the farm?
4. What has made Mr Hunt's farm so valuable?
5. Do you think the Canadians are really interested in buying the farm?
6. If you were Philip, what would you say to your father about selling the farm?

Write the answers in your exercise book.

2 Three houses for sale

These three houses are for sale. *Say which one you would like to live in and give reasons for your decision. Say what you don't like about the other two.*

3 Finding words

How many words can you find about buying, selling, building and doing business? ↓ ↑ → and ↘

c	d	e	b	t	a	z	b	p	y	c	x	d	w
o	x	v	u	f	u	g	t	l	h	x	i	y	j
m	z	k	s	a	l	b	w	a	m	b	v	c	n
p	d	m	i	l	l	i	o	n	s	p	a	e	q
a	f	d	n	r	g	s	r	n	h	t	l	n	i
n	u	j	e	v	j	w	t	i	k	b	u	y	k
y	x	l	s	a	x	m	h	n	z	n	a	a	o
b	p	c	s	a	l	e	q	g	g	d	b	r	e
s	p	f	t	g	u	h	v	i	e	w	l	j	x
p	e	r	m	i	s	s	i	o	n	k	e	y	l
z	m	a	o	n	b	o	c	p	e	d	q	e	r
f	s	g	n	f	t	h	u	i	r	v	j	s	k
l	y	m	e	z	i	n	a	o	o	f	f	e	r
b	p	c	y	q	d	t	r	e	u	s	f	l	t
g	u	h	v	i	w	j	x	k	s	y	l	l	z

1. _____
2. _____
3. _____
4. _____
5. _____
6. _____
7. _____
8. _____
9. _____
10. _____
11. _____
12. _____
13. _____
14. _____
15. _____

Kent: a fine place for the rich!

1 What would they say?

MP

Unemployed woman

Member of FoE

Rich local resident

Young local resident

Long-distance lorry driver

Write down what you think the following people would say about the motorway to the East London River Crossing.

1. _____

_____

2. _____

_____

3. _____

_____

4. _____

_____

5. _____

_____

6. _____

_____

early   hard   bad   serious   quick

certain   well   little   quick   soon

2 A theme park for Leaves Green

Some of the young people who live in Leaves Green are talking about the idea of the theme park. *Complete their conversation.*

Tom: Why didn't anyone think any _____ about a theme park for Leaves Green?

Carol: I don't know about you, Tom, but I could _____ believe my ears when I heard

about it yesterday.

Sam: The Hunts have _____ wanted to sell their farm for ages.

Tom: Yes, I know. They were hit _____ by the recent problems because they had to

borrow even more money from the bank to pay their debts.

Carol: But they have reacted _____ than anyone else in Leaves Green.

Joe: I wonder what Philip thinks about his father's idea. He _____ won't agree to it.

Linda: You know him _____ of all, Jimmy. What do you think he'll say?

50

Jimmy: I'm sure he knows _____ than we do, but I'm sure he won't agree.

Sam: Oh, come on, Jimmy! Philip wants to sell this farm _____ so that he can buy a larger

one up north.

Tom: There's nothing wrong in that, Sam, but I'm not sure you're right. He's going to come home

_____ so we can ask him.

3 Who?

Read the sentences and decide which group of people is being described. Write definitions in your English book using the noun. Write the sentences out again in your exercise book but add 'boy', 'girl', 'man', or 'woman' to each.

1. These have more money than they need and love to live in Kent.
2. They have to be very careful with their money and often live in ghettos.
3. This group needs a doctor or nurse to look after them.
4. They have no jobs to go to and they don't go to school either.
5. They sometimes have a dog to help them and they also use a stick.
6. They cannot listen to music or to what you are saying to them.
7. This group finds it difficult to use their arms and legs.
8. They have an arm or a leg or some other part of the body missing.

 A nasty surprise

1 Philip's opinion

When Philip arrived home, what do you think he said to his father and the Canadians who were with his father? *Write a short dialogue. These expressions will help you:*

I'm very disappointed…

You're cerainly making…

Sometimes I think you don't listen…

Why didn't you tell me…?

Don't just think about…

Whose idea was it…?

I've always wanted…

I only came home to…

Unit 6

2 At the hotel

Back at their hotel, the Canadians, Scott, Bill and
Eric, talked about the advantages and disadvantages
of buying Highams Hill Farm. **One** adverb is missing
in each sentence. *Choose the right adverb.*

Scott: Boy! What a terrible day we had today!

Bill: You're right, Scott. _____ I wonder

whether the old man wants to sell the farm.

Eric: Well, I don't _____ care.

Bill: Why not, Eric?

Eric: Well, I _____ don't think it's the right place for a theme park.

Scott: _____, I think you're right, Eric.

Bill: Now, listen! We'll _____ find a place like this for £2,000,000.

Eric: But if I had known _____ that there were so many environmentalists around here,

I wouldn't have flown over.

Scott: Eric's right. Hunt's son is going to make things even _____

Bill: I guess you're right. He _____ started a fight, didn't he?

Eric: Yes, but luckily he didn't. However, he could _____ cause a lot of trouble.

really sometimes certainly unfortunately never earlier more difficult nearly still

NIMBY at Leaves Green

1 True or false?

Correct the sentences in your exercise book if you think they are wrong.

1. You can listen to Radio Invicta all over Britain.
2. 'Environmental Watch' is a programme about pollution in Kent.
3. This programme is broadcast once a week.
4. Leaves Green is a pretty village in the East End of London.
5. No cars, buses or lorries could use the High Street because of a demonstration.
6. There were three groups at the meeting: Friends of the Earth, Council for the Preservation of Rural England and No Industry Made By Yuppies.
7. The Canadian company decided to buy part of Leaves Green because it is probably going to be close to the new Chunnel rail link.
8. 'Environmental Watch' was followed by a music programme.

2 NIMBY

Look at the pictures and say whether you would or would not be willing to have what you can see there in or near your back yard. Give reasons. Use your exercise book.

1 A crossword puzzle

ACROSS:

1. Small trees that grow round a garden or field.
6. Short form of a word or name.
12. A measure of land.
13. You need this to be able to do things like reading a book.
14. Showing 'where'.
15. Short form for 'California'.
16. A group of sentences in a text.
21. To move something from 'here' to 'there'.
22. More than 'tens' but not 'thousands'.
23. A simple present form of 'to be'.
25. An emergency.
27. You can buy something with a … card.
28. Opposite of 'no'.
29. Plants need this to grow.
31. You may say this when you leave a friend.
32. What you think or feel about something.
33. Italians (and others) love to eat this.
35. Short form of 'for example'.
36. It is either you … me!
37. You write this on a letter so that it arrives safely.
40. 1st person singular present of 'to be'.
41. You have these if you borrow money.
44. Another word for 'because'.
45. People often live in this when they are on holiday.
47. For this reason.
48. To see if you can do something or not.
50. You use it to keep paper, wood, etc. together.
52. Part of a city but not the centre.
55. One of two.
56. To move very quickly from one place to another.
57. Indefinite article used in front of vowels.
58. They play football together.
59. To speak or do something for another person.
60. It is built across a river or a road.

DOWN:

1. Two of these are on the end of your arms.
2. Many of the countries of Europe have joined together to make this.
3. He/She makes a picture with a pen or pencil.
4. To buy or take something.
5. California is one.
6. Can live on land and in water.
7. A very nice person to look at.
8. Waiting to go.
9. Name of a group of high mountains.
10. Personal pronoun for 'things'.
11. Not used before.
15. To say angry words to someone.
17. Short for 'Royal Navy'.
18. They're the best.
19. What is left of your dinner, for example.
20. Short for 'advertisements'.
21. Short for 'Personal Computer'.
23. Short for 'I owe you'.
24. Not front or back.
26. Verb of the adjective 'oppressive'.
29. No curves or bends in the road, perhaps.
30. Part of your body that you use for walking.
33. They drink a lot of this in U.S.A.
34. Sometimes thousands of people live and work in these.
38. You open it when you go into a room.
39. Telling someone something.
42. Part of a theatre.
43. To do with the countryside.
46. To go in a different direction.
47. Light and heat come from it.
49. You need a book to be able to do this.
51. His first name is 'Samuel'.
53. Another word for 'however'.
54. Place where adults go for a drink.

A Superstar

if
and so
because
and
yet
who
when
before
although
but

1 Meet Felix Hart

1. Felix Hart is an English actor…
2. He is part of America's city life,…
3. Felix became an actor…
4. In England he was very successful in plays…
5. But he give up his career on the stage…
6. At the beginning, life in America was very difficult for him…
7. The Tarzan pictures he made in Florida were not very good…
8. His 'bread and honey' commercials were well paid…
9. He had to work hard…
10. He would not have become an American citizen…

a) …his parents had different ideas about his future.
b) …he was offered a part in a film.
c) …they gave people a lot of pleasure.
d) …he had not liked the country and the people.
e) …now lives and works in America.
f) …he was able to buy a house in Vermont.
g) …he prefers to spend his time in a lonely place in Florida.
h) …his first film was not successful.
i) …London's audiences loved him.
j) …he became Hollywood's superstar.

2 Computer errors

Mandy Fling, film director, wanted to do a TV documentary on Felix Hart. After she had put down her ideas in her computer notebook, she found that the commas, full stops, apostrophes, etc. were missing.
Put them back in the text again and write it in your exercise book.

InthisdocumentaryIdnotonlyliketotalkaboutFelixsbigfilmswhichmadehimsofamousbutalsoaboutthedays

inhislifewhenhewasayoungboyandayoungmaninoneofLondonssuburbsWecouldforexampleshowthe

childrensplaygroundsandtheboysschoolhewenttoOfcourseweshouldalsointerviewhisparentsImsure

hisparentsplansforhimwouldinteresteverybodyastheresalsoalessontobelearntYesterdaysdreamsarehardly

evertodaysfactsSoinsteadofbeingoneofBritainsmanybankmanagersFelixhasbecomeoneoftheworldssuper

starsWemustnthoweverforgetthatweregoingtoproducethisdocumentaryforAmericastelevisionaudiences

TheydcertainlylovetohearaboutHollywoodsimportanceforthefilmindustryanditsgreatculturalachieve

mentthereItsnotonlyafilmaboutFelixspartsinsomeofShakespearesplaysbutalsoaboutourcountrysmodern

historyandtheroleanEnglishactorhasplayedandisstillplayinginit

3 Farewell tea party

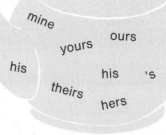

Mr Wynne invited a group of German exchange students
to his house together with their British hosts. Here is
what some of the German students said.

1. Oh, excuse me. I think we've mixed up our glasses. This one here
   is my glass and that one over there must be your glass.
2. Mrs Wynne, I like the apple tree at the back of the garden. At home
   we've got one, too. An apple tree, I mean. But it's much smaller.
3. How can you sort out all the CDs afterwards? I know, Peter has put his name on his disks, and Judy and
   Jane have brought some, too. They left them in the corner over there. But are they really all their disks?
   There seem to be so many.
4. I quite liked the break dance that Peggy and Walter did. Their performance was super, wasn't it? However,
   I preferred his performance to Peggy's performance.
5. Sometimes it's quite difficult to understand you all. John's accent is definitely Welsh and Brian's accent
   could be northern. I haven't yet decided on Joan's accent. Could her accent be Scottish?

Whenever possible, use different ways to express possession*. Do this exercise in your exercise book.

possession [pə'zeʃn] – Besitz, Zugehörigkeit

B Advertising

1 A party in Florida

At a party at Felix Hart's house in Florida one of his friends said to various groups of guests: "Most English
actors who come over to America can look forward to a brilliant career in the film industry, can't they?"
Here are the reactions of the guests:

Shorten the first part of the answers. Use your exercise book.
Example: 1. It seems so.

It seems to be a bit like that. Fiona Leigh and Cary Long
are doing quite well at the moment. And they're English,
aren't they!

I think that's right. They are all very successful.

I hope that's not true. Just imagine James Went earning
millions of dollars over here. He can't act at all.

I'm afraid that's quite wrong. Jane Farrell,
who is really great, can't get any parts at all.

If that's the case, why do only a few come over then?

I suppose that's true. It's probably because most of them have acted on the stage.

I would say the same. There's hardly anybody who's not made it to the top.

Yes. If they don't become big stars, it's only because they don't stay over here long enough.

I don't think you can say that. We only hear of the successful actors, never of the ones who don't make it!

2 A break at Rebecca's training programme

Who talked to whom?

1. Is Felix Hart really English? I thought he was American.

2. Are there commercials on German TV, too?

3. Did Richard Burton or Felix Hart play Nero in the Hollywood movie 'Quo Vadis'?

4. I've never seen any of Felix Hart's commercials.

5. Can you remember the first rule of advertising?

6. Arnold Schwarzenegger believes that an actor has to publicize himself.

7. Is Felix Hart still doing commercials?

8. I'm sure Felix Hart will never move back to England.

9. So what's your field in advertising? Means of transport? Cars, trucks, or motorbikes?

10. Arnold Schwarzenegger doesn't want to hide the fact that he's from Europe.

a) None of them. I'm doing ads for clothes at the moment.

b) No, he isn't.

c) So did I.

d) Sorry. No, I can't.

e) Yes, there are.

f) Nor does Felix Hart.

g) Of course he will.

h) So do most actors.

i) Neither of them did. It was Peter Ustinov.

j) Neither have I.

1. _____ 2. _____ 3. _____ 4. _____ 5. _____ 6. _____ 7. _____ 8. _____ 9. _____ 10. _____

C [The street to the stars]

1 Sunset Boulevard

It goes north, so start at the bottom. Use the correct forms of the verbs and fill in the proper names.

to start

to go on to   to leave

to reach   to enter   to pass through

to go down   to go through   not to finish   to go to past   to continue

9. Finally, after 24 miles, it _____ a point where the Pacific Ocean can be seen.

8. It also _____ a place where a lot of young people study.

7. Then it _____ past lovely mansions with swimming pools and tennis courts.

6. It _____ there but _____ an area which is the home of many film stars.

5. Next it _____ a canyon of nightclubs, restaurants and huge ads.

4. Having _____ this suburb, it _____ to a famous place with a lot of film studios.

3. Then it _____ a beautiful suburb.

2. After that it _____ some immigrant communities.

1. It _____ in the city of Los Angeles.

_____

_____

_____

_____

_____

_____

_____

_____

Downtown LA

2 Not quite sure

Here is what Cindy knows about Arnold Schwarzenegger:
He came to the States in the late seventies.
He had problems at first because he had not learned to speak English without an accent.
He would have improved his English after a time because he is quick to learn.
A business career had also been a possibility for him.
In Austria he had always thought about becoming a sports teacher.

When talking to Brian, she is quite careful. She uses modal constructions to express that she is not quite sure. What might she have said? *Use the following modals:* might, needn't, should, could, must.

Brian: When did Arnold come over to the States for the first time?

Cindy: That __*he must have come to the States in the late seventies*__

because the first bodybuilding championship took place then, and Arnold took part in them.

Brian: You know Arnold quite well, don't you? What advice would you have given him before going to America?

Cindy: He _____

_____

It would have made things much easier for him at the beginning of his career.

Brian: Arnold went to language classes, accent classes, voice classes… Was that really necessary?

Cindy: No, he _____

You see, he would have learned most of it through his contacts. But going to classes was much quicker.

Brian: Were there a lot of jobs open to him, or was there only bodybuilding or acting?

Cindy: No, he _____

He isn't just good at one thing, you know.

Brian: And what if he had stayed in Austria?

Cindy: That's difficult to say. I don't think he would have taken up acting. I think _____

_____

because he likes to work with people.

The trip to Vermont

1 Mum's last words

In the end, Lucy's mother packs her suitcases. Before Lucy flies to America, her mum tells her once again where everything is packed, what she should remember and what she should be careful about. *What did she say?*

1 "Listen, Lucy! The United States _____ not like England. The cities _____ really

dangerous and the police _____ deal with a lot of street crime. So do be careful where you keep

your money. Perhaps it would be best just to have $10 in your pocket. If $10 _____ stolen, it's not

the world.

Don't forget to tell Aunt Vanessa that Martin is doing physics at Oxford University. Physics _____ her husband's subject at university years ago. He also once wanted to do economics, but then he decided that economics _____ too dry for him.

But the way, I've have packed your cases very carefully. This small one has everything you need if the big one gets lost. You never know with these airlines. Here _____ your nice blue jeans. Your pyjamas _____ in the side pocket and your second _____ of glasses _____ on top of everything, next to your toilet bag.

In the big brown case you'll find everything that you don't need every day: new clothes, like your black trousers. They _____ so expensive when we bought _____ at Lewis's, you should really only wear _____ on special days. Be careful when you unpack. Wrapped in your pullovers _____ your dad's binoculars. _____ will break easily if you drop _____.

Well, I think we'll have to leave soon. Unfortunately, the travel news on the radio _____ bad all day. The information about the M4 _____ that it is blocked. Their advice _____ terrible: take the country roads instead! But if everybody does that, we'll never get to the airport!"

"Oh, Mum! Everything will be OK. We'll get there in time!"

2 In the plane

Here are some of the things that happened just before Lucy's plane took off* from London to New York.

1. Lucy's heart beat faster.
2. Some people put out their cigarettes.
3. Most people fastened their seat belts.
4. Lucy's mouth got all dry.
5. The captain gave information about the flight.
6. The plane moved slowly away from the airport building.
7. The noise of the engines got louder.
8. Cold fear crept up Lucy's body.
9. Some people closed their eyes.
10. The plane shook a bit.
11. The airport building became smaller.

Write down what Lucy heard, listened to, felt, watched and saw happening in the plane just before she took off for New York. Use your exercise book.

* to take off – starten

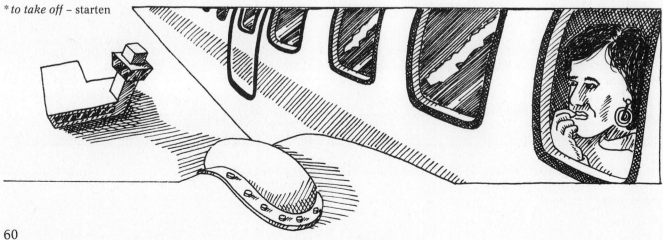

3 Life in Lucy's family

Lucy is talking to her American relatives about her family.

"My parents are really OK. I'm allowed to go out until 11 o'clock at night. We used to have problems with our garden and our car, though. My parents wanted me and my brother Martin to do the garden and clean the car. But we didn't have any time for that. So they decided to get somebody to cut the grass and to clean the car once a week. Of course, we've got to do something. We have to clean our own rooms and help in the kitchen. I hate that because there are nicer things in life than washing up dirty dishes.
They don't say anything when we turn up our radios or when we invite our friends for the evening. But the TV programmes! When there's a football match on, you can't watch your favourite programme. My father and my mother are both keen football fans!
Dad always finds somebody to repair our bikes. The other day I told him that my light wasn't working and two days later a new light had been put on. Who was it? I don't know, but certainly not dad!
They might change, of course! They might tell me to cook the Sunday dinner, they mightn't allow Martin to drive dad's car any more if he doesn't wash it and they might even think of changing the lock on the front door if we keep on coming home after 11 o'clock at night!"

What does Lucy say about her parents' attitude towards her brother Martin and herself? Use 'make', 'let', and 'have'. Write the sentences in your exercise book. Consider the following points:

[An explosion of laughter]

1 Another megastar: Jody Foster

Since the arrival of talking pictures more than 100,000 actresses have played roles in Hollywood movies, but only 11 women have won Oscars for Best Actress more than once. The last woman to do this was Jody Foster in 1993.

Who is Jody Foster? She was born on November 19, 1962 as the fourth child of Lucius Foster and Evelyn Foster. Unfortunately her father left the family four months before Jody was born. So he has never been important for her; she says that she has only seen him four times in her life.

Her mother had to look after the four children and she did a good job. On the one hand, she helped develop their natural talents; on the other hand, she made them get a first-class education. So Jody started to act in commercials when she was three years old and later – in her teens – she regularly played girls' parts in movies. But she also went to one of the best schools in California and graduated* in American literature at Yale University.

So far, Jody has mostly played working-class women of little education, who were losers** in society. Hollywood's film directors believe that this is really one of her strong points. Or will she – in future – play the roles of more successful women as she did in 'Sommersby', the film that came out in 1993? Or will she even make films?

We know only very little about her personal life. The newspapers usually leave her alone. Articles about her, however, tell us that she speaks French perfectly, stays very close to her mother and lives alone in a middle-class home in the neighbourhood of San Fernando Valley.

* *to graduate* ['grædju:eit] – einen akademischen Grad erlangen
**loser ['lu:zə] – Verlierer(in), Versager(in)

Read the text carefully and then ask questions about it.
Examples: How many actresses have played roles in Hollywood movies?
            When was Jody Foster born?
Write ten more questions in your exercise book.

2 Building words

1. *Make a list of a) the prefixes b) the suffixes and c) the roots.*
2. *Make as many words as you can.*

care
un   wait   act   less   er
argue   ress   hope
happy   logic   ence
agree   appear   ful   help
or   interest   ful
use   ment   depend
comfort   ness   able
invent   differ   ance
al   direct   ing
dis   use   ion
ion   in   ence   il

_____

_____

_____

_____

_____

⟨3 Phrases for tourists⟩

Hier sind einige Sätze aus einem Sprachbuch für Touristen. Übersetze sie ins Englische.

a) Im Motel
   1. Ich kann meine Hose nicht mehr finden. Sie war hier auf dem Stuhl.
   2. Das sind nicht meine Socken. Meine sind grau.
   3. Ich habe immer noch kein eigenes Zimmer.
   4. Ich habe es mir anders überlegt.
   5. Wissen Sie, wo mein Fernglas ist?

b) Ein Unfall
   1. Er ist sicher zu schnell gefahren.
   2. Bei diesem Unfall starben zwei Menschen.
   3. Man hätte einen Krankenwagen rufen müssen.
   4. Die Polizei war sehr vorsichtig und hielt den Verkehr eine Viertelstunde an.
   5. Was hätte ich tun können?

c) Vor dem Fernseher
   1. Was sind die neuesten Nachrichten aus Deutschland?
   2. Die Informationen über Deutschland sind nicht sehr gut.
   3. Die Vereinigten Staaten haben wieder Probleme mit einer Raumfähre*.
   4. Könnten Sie mir meine Brille geben? Ohne sie kann ich nichts sehen.

* Raumfähre – *space shuttle*

When will I become a steak?

Never, I hope, sir!

4 Be your own scriptwriter

a) *You know what a script looks like. Now write the first twelve 'takes' of a script of your own. Use the present tense. Don't forget to use phrases like* credits start, fade in, pull back, cut to, end of opening credits, *etc.*
The script could be about a) life at an English school b) a mining disaster c) a refugee from a Third World country or d) an adventure story.

1. _____
   _____

2. _____
   _____

3. _____
   _____

4. _____
   _____

5. _____
   _____

6. _____
   _____

7. _____
   _____

8. _____
   _____

9. _____
   _____

10. _____
    _____

11. _____
    _____

12. _____
    _____

b) *Now tell the story of what happened in the past tense. Use your exercise book.*